INTRODUCTION

Join Puff on a National Park Adventure!

Hi there, Explorer!

Meet Puff, a friendly little pup with a BIG sense of adventure! But Puff isn't just any dog—he's a pilot, and he's ready to take you on an unforgettable journey through all 63 U.S. National Parks!

From the rocky shores of Acadia to the towering cliffs of Zion, Puff is on a mission to explore the wild, wonderful places that make our country so special. Along the way, you'll discover fun facts, learn about amazing animals and landscapes, and bring each park to life with your own colors and creativity.

Whether you're at home, in the car, or camping under the stars, this book is your passport to adventure. So grab your favorite coloring tools, climb aboard Puff's little red plane, and get ready to color, learn + explore the beauty of nature—one park at a time.

Let's go—it's time to travel with Puff!

ACADIA NATIONAL PARK (MAINE)

Rise and shine! Acadia is one of the first places in the U.S. to see the sunrise—early birds, this one's for you!

ARCHES NATIONAL PARK (UTAH)

Rock on! Arches has over 2,000 stone arches—nature's way of playing with building blocks!

Badlands National Park (South Dakota)

Dino-mite! The Badlands is like a giant treasure chest for fossils—scientists have found ancient rhinos and saber-toothed cats here!

Big Bend National Park (Texas)

Starlight, star bright! Look up—Big Bend has some of the darkest skies in the U.S., perfect for stargazing!

Biscayne National Park (Florida)

Splish, splash! Biscayne is mostly underwater—imagine a whole national park just for fish and sea turtles!

BLACK CANYON OF THE GUNNISON NATIONAL PARK (COLORADO)

Peek-a-boo, sun! Some parts of this canyon only get 33 minutes of sunlight a day—it's like nature's hide-and-seek!

BRYCE CANYON NATIONAL PARK (UTAH)

Rock castles galore! Bryce is filled with weird rock towers called "hoodoos" that look like a fairy tale kingdom!

CANYONLANDS NATIONAL PARK (UTAH)

Picture-perfect! The famous Mesa Arch glows like it's on fire when the sun rises—nature's magic trick!

CAPITOL REEF NATIONAL PARK (UTAH)

Ancient doodles! This park has rock carvings made by Native Americans over 1,000 years ago—talk about old-school graffiti!

Carlsbad Caverns National Park (New Mexico)

Bat-tastic! Every evening, thousands of bats zoom out of the cave like a spooky flying parade!

CHANNEL ISLANDS NATIONAL PARK (CALIFORNIA)

Tiny but mighty! The adorable island fox is smaller than a house cat and only lives here—VIP (Very Important Paws)!

Congaree National Park (South Carolina)

Giant trees ahead! Some trees in Congaree are as tall as a 17-story building—imagine climbing that treehouse!

CRATER LAKE NATIONAL PARK (OREGON)

No rivers allowed! Crater Lake is the deepest lake in the U.S., and it's made entirely of rain and snow—nature's biggest water bottle!

CUYAHOGA VALLEY NATIONAL PARK (OHIO)

All aboard! This park has a scenic train ride, waterfalls, and lush forests right near the city—nature and adventure rolled into one!

DEATH VALLEY NATIONAL PARK (CALIFORNIA & NEVADA)

Hot, hot, hot! Death Valley holds the record for the hottest temperature ever recorded on Earth—134°F! Bring your sunscreen (and lots of water)!

DENALI NATIONAL PARK (ALASKA)

Sky-high alert! Denali is home to the tallest mountain in North America—so tall it makes clouds look low!

DRY TORTUGAS NATIONAL PARK (FLORIDA)

Pirate vibes only! You can only reach this island park by boat or seaplane—and it's home to a massive old fort surrounded by crystal blue water!

EVERGLADES NATIONAL PARK (FLORIDA)

Swamp surprise! The Everglades is the only place in the world where alligators and crocodiles live side by side!

GATES OF THE ARCTIC NATIONAL PARK (ALASKA)

No roads, no trails! This wild park is so remote, the only way in is by plane or a serious wilderness hike—total explorer territory!

GATEWAY ARCH NATIONAL PARK (MISSOURI)

Arch you glad? This park has a 630-foot tall stainless steel arch—the tallest in the world—and you can ride an elevator to the top!

GLACIER NATIONAL PARK (MONTANA)

Road trip alert! The famous Going-to-the-Sun Road winds through snowy peaks and alpine lakes—it's one unforgettable drive!

GLACIER BAY NATIONAL PARK (ALASKA)

Icy action! Watch glaciers move, crack, and splash into the sea—like nature's slow-motion waterfall show!

GRAND CANYON NATIONAL PARK (ARIZONA)

Whoa! This canyon is over a mile deep and 277 miles long—so big it can even make a mountain look small!

GRAND TETON NATIONAL PARK (WYOMING)

Sharp peaks ahead! The Tetons rise suddenly from flat land, like a giant surprise party for mountain lovers.

GREAT BASIN NATIONAL PARK (NEVADA)

Cave crawling and star gazing! You can explore marble caves underground and see millions of stars at night—all in one park.

GREAT SAND DUNES NATIONAL PARK (COLORADO)

Sand for days! This park has the tallest sand dunes in North America—you can even sled down them like snowy hills!

GREAT SMOKY MOUNTAINS NATIONAL PARK (TENNESSEE & NORTH CAROLINA)

Misty magic! The Smokies get their name from the fog that rolls through the trees—it looks like smoke drifting over the mountains.

GUADALUPE MOUNTAINS NATIONAL PARK (TEXAS)

Top of Texas! This park has the tallest mountain in the state—and a fossil reef from an ancient ocean!

HALEAKALĀ NATIONAL PARK (HAWAI'I)

Sunrise from the stars! Watching the sunrise from this giant volcano feels like you're standing on Mars—or the Moon! ancient ocean!

HAWAI'I VOLCANOES NATIONAL PARK (HAWAI'I)

Lava love! This park has two of the world's most active volcanoes—where you might even see lava flowing!

HOT SPRINGS NATIONAL PARK (ARKANSAS)

Soak it up! People have been coming to these warm, natural springs for hundreds of years—nature's original spa!

INDIANA DUNES NATIONAL PARK (INDIANA)

Beach vibes in the Midwest! This park has sand dunes you can climb and splashy waves from Lake Michigan!

ISLE ROYALE NATIONAL PARK (MICHIGAN)

Island mystery! No cars, no crowds—just moose and wolves living wild on this remote island in the middle of a Great Lake.

JOSHUA TREE NATIONAL PARK (CALIFORNIA)

Twist and shout! This desert park is full of wacky-looking Joshua trees—like Dr. Seuss plants come to life!

KATMAI NATIONAL PARK (ALASKA)

Bear alert! Katmai is one of the best places to watch brown bears catching salmon right out of the river—snack time!

KENAI FJORDS NATIONAL PARK (ALASKA)

Ice, ice, baby! Massive glaciers carve deep valleys into the land—and sea otters float nearby like fuzzy boats!

KINGS CANYON NATIONAL PARK (CALIFORNIA)

Deep and dramatic! Kings Canyon has one of the deepest canyons in the U.S.—even deeper than the Grand Canyon in some spots!

KOBUK VALLEY NATIONAL PARK (ALASKA)

Sandy surprise! This park is home to Arctic sand dunes—yes, real dunes in the far north, where caribou roam the ridges.

Lake Clark National Park (Alaska)

Volcano views and wild lakes! You might see bears fishing, salmon leaping, and even steaming volcanoes in the distance!

LASSEN VOLCANIC NATIONAL PARK (CALIFORNIA)

Bubble, bubble, mudpot trouble! Lassen is full of steaming vents and boiling mud—like a giant, natural science lab!

MAMMOTH CAVE NATIONAL PARK (KENTUCKY)

Mammoth Cave is the longest cave system in the whole world — it's like an underground maze with over 400 miles of tunnels! That's longer than 7,000 football fields lined up!

MESA VERDE NATIONAL PARK (COLORADO)

Cliff dwellers! This park protects ancient homes built into cliffs by Native Americans over 700 years ago.

MOUNT RAINIER NATIONAL PARK (WASHINGTON)

Snowy giant! Mount Rainier is a volcano covered in glaciers and wildflowers—it's the tallest peak in the state!

NEW RIVER GORGE NATIONAL PARK (WEST VIRGINIA)

Bridge bragging rights! This park's huge arch bridge is one of the longest of its kind—you can even walk across it during Bridge Day!

NORTH CASCADES NATIONAL PARK (WASHINGTON)

The Alps of America! With over 300 glaciers and jagged peaks, this wild park looks like it belongs in a fairy tale.

OLYMPIC NATIONAL PARK (WASHINGTON)

Triple treat! Olympic has snow-capped mountains, lush rainforests, and wild beaches—all in one amazing park!

PETRIFIED FOREST NATIONAL PARK (ARIZONA)

Stone trees? Yep! This desert park is full of ancient trees turned to colorful stone—nature's own crystal collection.

PINNACLES NATIONAL PARK (CALIFORNIA)

Rocky and batty! Climb spiky rock formations by day, and spot bats flying out of caves at sunset.

REDWOOD NATIONAL AND STATE PARKS (CALIFORNIA)

Tallest trees on Earth! Redwoods can grow over 350 feet tall—so high you can barely see the tops!

Rocky Mountain National Park (Colorado)

Breathe deep! This park reaches sky-high elevations, with roads and trails climbing over 12,000 feet.

SAGUARO NATIONAL PARK (ARIZONA)

Cactus central! Saguaro is home to the famous tall, spiky cactus—some live for 200 years and grow taller than houses!

SEQUOIA NATIONAL PARK (CALIFORNIA)

Giant alert! This park has the biggest trees in the world by volume—so big you could walk through one!

SHENANDOAH NATIONAL PARK (VIRGINIA)

Skyline cruising! Take a drive on Skyline Drive and soak in the mountain views, waterfalls, and wildflowers.

THEODORE ROOSEVELT NATIONAL PARK (NORTH DAKOTA)

Bison and badlands! This wild park has herds of bison roaming the colorful hills—just like in cowboy days!

VIRGIN ISLANDS NATIONAL PARK
(U.S. VIRGIN ISLANDS)

Tropical treasure! Swim in clear blue water, snorkel over coral reefs, and explore ruins of old sugar plantations.

VOYAGEURS NATIONAL PARK (MINNESOTA)

Boat life! This watery park is full of lakes and islands—you'll need a canoe or kayak to explore it all!

WHITE SANDS NATIONAL PARK (NEW MEXICO)

Snowy sand? The dunes here are bright white and made of gypsum—it looks like winter, but it's warm desert!

WIND CAVE NATIONAL PARK (SOUTH DAKOTA)

Hidden maze! Wind Cave has some of the world's longest and most unique passageways—named for the wind that rushes out!

WRANGELL–ST. ELIAS NATIONAL PARK (ALASKA)

America's largest! This park is bigger than some states—it's filled with glaciers, volcanoes, and towering mountains!

YELLOWSTONE NATIONAL PARK (WYOMING, MONTANA, IDAHO)

Geyser countdown! Yellowstone's Old Faithful shoots boiling water into the sky like clockwork—every 90 minutes or so!

YOSEMITE NATIONAL PARK (CALIFORNIA)

Waterfall wonder! Yosemite Falls is one of the tallest in North America—and the granite cliffs are epic too!

Zion National Park (Utah)

Canyon adventure! Hike through narrow river canyons and red rock cliffs so tall they block the sky!

DID YOU KNOW?

The very first U.S. national park was **Yellowstone**, created all the way back in **1872**!

Today, there are **63 official national parks** across the country, each one protecting amazing places like waterfalls, volcanoes, coral reefs, deserts, and glaciers.

That's **63** adventures waiting just for you!

DESIGN YOUR OWN NATIONAL PARK!

What would your dream park look like?
Draw mountains, trees, animals, or even something totally magical.
This is your space—make it wild and wonderful!

THANKS FOR COLORING WITH US

We'd love to see your art!
Ask a grown-up to share your finished pages with us @momobookscoloring and use #ColorWithPuff to join the adventure! Let's keep creating together.

www.ingramcontent.com/pod-product-compliance
Lightning Source LLC
Chambersburg PA
CBHW040004040426
42337CB00033B/5219